T0084992

Fall Field Trips

Let's Go to the
Apple
Orchard

by Lisa J. Amstutz

PEBBLE
a capstone imprint

Pebble Emerge is published by Pebble, an imprint of Capstone.
1710 Roe Crest Drive
North Mankato, Minnesota 56003
www.capstonepub.com

Copyright © 2021 by Capstone. All rights reserved. No part of this publication may be reproduced in whole or in part, or stored in a retrieval system, or transmitted in any form or by any means, electronic, mechanical, photocopying, recording, or otherwise, without written permission of the publisher.

Library of Congress Cataloging-in-Publication Data is available on the Library of Congress website.
ISBN 978-1-9771-2447-0 (library binding)
ISBN 978-1-9771-2490-6 (eBook PDF)

Summary: It's fall, and it's time to visit the apple orchard! Take a close look at apple trees, learn how to pick apples, and have some fun pressing apples too. Through playful text and beautiful images, kids will experience what it's like to visit an apple orchard.

Image Credits
Capstone Press: Gary Sundermeyer, 10; Capstone Studio: Karon Dubke, 20; iStockphoto: hanapon1002, Cover; Shutterstock: Africa Studio, 1, agrofruti, 6, Artefficient, design element, Bufo, 14, 15, EvgeniiAnd, 9, grey_and, 7, lammotos, 18, images72, 5, Jaren Jai Wicklund, 16, jullyromas, 2, Marc Bruxelle, 17, Nella, 3, Romiana Lee, 4, RonGreer.Com, 19, solarus, design element, TairA, 11, Thomas Oswald, 13, Vectorchoice, design element

Editorial Credits
Editor: Shelly Lyons; Designer: Kayla Rossow; Media Researcher: Morgan Walters; Production Specialist: Spencer Rosio

All internet sites appearing in back matter were available and accurate when this book was sent to press.

Printed and bound in China
PO3322

Table of Contents

Words in **bold** are in the glossary.

A Trip to the Orchard

Summer is over. The air is cooler now. Fall is here. The leaves are red, orange, and brown. Apples are ready to pick. It is time to visit the apple orchard!

An orchard is a field of trees. The trees are planted in neat rows. Fruit or nuts grow on the trees. An apple orchard's trees grow apples.

How Do Apples Grow?

Apple trees grow flowers in spring. In summer, the flowers turn into apples. The apples start out small. They grow and grow!

pulp

seed pocket

Inside each apple are five seed pockets.
An apple's stem and seeds are called
the core. The core is not good to eat.
But an apple's juicy white **pulp** is tasty.

At the Orchard

We are here! Look at the big wagon. A tractor pulls it. Let's take a ride! We sit on blocks of straw called bales. A farmer drives the tractor slowly. Down a trail we go. There is lots to see! Hold on! The ride is bumpy.

The orchard is a busy place. Workers pick apples. They reach high into the trees. Big boxes hold the picked apples.

We taste all kinds of apples. Each kind is called a **variety**. Some apples are sweet, and others are **tart**. *Crunch!* Some are **crisp**, and others are soft.

What is that yummy smell? Someone is making cider! Cider is a drink made from apples. You can drink it warm or cold.

We toss some apples in the cider **press**. Then we turn the handle. *Squish!* The machine **smashes** the apples. Juice runs out into a glass.

There is so much to do at the orchard!
We see animals in the barn. The pony
munches on hay. Pigs squeal and snort.
They like to eat apples.

Next to the barn is a face-painting booth. A woman paints faces. We will look like animals. Should we choose a bear? A tiger? How about a giraffe?

Picking and Eating Apples

It is almost time to go home. But first, let's pick some apples! Lift and twist the fruit. The fruit will easily pop off its stem.

There are many kinds of apples. Some turn red when they are **ripe**. Others turn yellow or green. Let's pick some of each.

Now we make applesauce. First we **peel** the apples. Next we cut out the cores. Then we cook the apples and mash them. We'll add some **cinnamon**. Yum!

Apples are used to make other good food too. Muffins and pies are made with apples. Caramel apples are a sweet treat. What is your favorite way to eat apples?

Apple Prints

Did you know that an apple has a star inside?
Try making apple prints to see for yourself!

What You Need:

- apples
- knife
- paintbrush
- paint
- paper

What You Do:

1. Ask an adult to cut an apple in half around the middle.

2. Use the paintbrush to paint a cut side of the apple.

3. Press the painted apple onto a piece of paper. Let the print dry. Can you see the star?

Glossary

cinnamon (SIN-uh-muhn)—a reddish-brown spice that comes from the inner bark of a tree

crisp (KRISP)—firm and easily broken

peel (PEEL)—to remove the skin from a vegetable or fruit

press (PRESS)—a machine used to crush apples to make cider

pulp (PUHLP)—the fleshy part of a fruit

ripe (RIPE)—ready to pick and eat

smash (SMASH)—to break something into many small pieces

tart (TART)—sour-tasting

variety (vuh-RYE-i-tee)—a type of plant that is different from others of its kind

Read More

Anderson, Steve. *From Seed to Apple Tree.* Minneapolis: Cantata Learning, 2016.

Clark, Rosalyn. *A Visit to the Orchard.* Minneapolis: Lerner, 2018.

Gleisner, Jenna Lee. *Apple Harvest.* Mankato, MN: Child's World, 2017.

Internet Links

Apple Fun Facts
https://www.appleholler.com/orchard-farm/all-about-apples/apple-fun-facts/

Fun Apple Facts
https://www.applesfromny.com/about/fun-facts

Index